ONiONS

What would civilization be without the onion! In one form or another, its flavor blends into virtually any part of any meal. Here are fabulous recipes for every kind of onion: yellow, red, Bermuda, Spanish, silverskins, pearl, scallions. Standbys such as "Onion Soup Gratiné", "Creamed Onions" and "French-Fried Onion Rings" are included together with marvelous innovations such as "Onions and Celery Avgolemono" (an appetizer), "Onions and Raisins" (a sweet hors-d'oeuvre), and "Onions Stuffed with Chicken Livers" (a unique main dish or accompaniment). A fine collection of dishes for one of our least expensive vegetables.

secrets of vegetable cooking
. . . is a series of attractive, low-priced cookbooks, each concerned with a specific vegetable and, most important, each containing a collection of more than 50 distinctive and delicious recipes for the broadest range of vegetable dishes. A special treat—the soup to nuts of vegetable cookery.

Inez M. Krech, author of the entire series, is well known as a writer (she was the co-author of "Naturally Italian") and as the editor of more than 200 cookbooks. She lives in New Jersey.

secrets of vegetable cookin

Inquiries should be addressed to
Crown Publishers, Inc., One Park Avenue, New York, New York 10016

Printed in the United States of America

Published simultaneously in
Canada by General Publishing Company Limited

Library of Congress Cataloging in Publication Data

Krech, Inez M.
    Onions.

    (Secrets of vegetable cooking)
    1. Cookery (Onions) I. Title. II. Series: Krech,
Inez M. Secrets of vegetable cooking.
TX803.O5K73   641.6'525   81-5580
ISBN 0-517-54444-X   AACR2

10 9 8 7 6 5 4 3 2 1
First edition

DESIGN AND COVER PHOTOGRAPH BY ALBERT SQUILLACE

ONiONS

by inez m. krech

primavera books   crown publishers, inc. / new york

Introduction

The onion family supplies the favorite flavoring vegetables for cooks the world over. The same genus, related to the lily, includes chives, scallions, leeks, garlic, shallots, yellow, white and red onions. The blossoms of our edible onions are small, like clusters of miniature lilies. Some species, under the name Allium, which is the genus name for onions, have been developed for their flowers. In classical times the onion was used for medicine as well as food; perhaps the good effects came from the minerals and vitamin C content (that was before the days of morning orange juice). Going back even further, the onion was deified in Ancient Egypt, where a mummy carried a bouquet of onions in his hands to help him get through the afterworld. Times have changed and we worship other things.

Chives, scallions and leeks are sold fresh, with green leaves. All the other onions are sold "cured" or dried. When they reach maturity, before they start to flower, they are bent over just above the bulb, and dried in windrows. The necks are fully dried before the onions are put into storage, and tops and roots are clipped off. In Italian red onions and sometimes other species, the tops are retained and used to make a braid; long braids of the onions are hung up to dry. The outer layer (or layers) of the onion dries to a thin papery skin; within this the other layers retain their juicy fleshy plumpness.

All these dried onions are still alive, like flower bulbs, and contain within them new onion plants. If you store an onion until the growing season, you will see the start of the new plant in a shoot, sometimes multiple shoots, from the center of the onion. The shoots are edible, but the layers of onion just around the shoots are usually soft since they are giving food to the new plant.

Scallions are baby or teenage onions of the same species. To begin with, farmers plant onion seeds; as the seeds germinate and reach a width at the base of about 1/3 inch, they are pulled and bunched for scallions before the base has begun to swell into bulb shape; they have the same width from base to top. (Or the tiny onions are bent over and dried to make "onion sets"; in the next spring these are sold to farmers and gardeners as the first stage in growing larger onions. This system makes it possible to grow large onions within the normal growing season in the Temperate Zone.) Scallions, being fresh, need to be refrigerated. They will keep for a few days in good condition, but if you store them for longer, you will need to peel off more of the drying outer layers to prepare them. Scallions are a very ancient form of onion. The name comes from <u>ascalonia caepa</u>, or onion of Ascalon. Ascalon, 12 miles north of Gaza, was a city of the Canaanites and was well known to the Egyptians and Romans. Actually, the Ascalon onion was the shallot, but over the years the names got confused. Even today some people call scallions shallots and vice versa. A more common name for the scallion is "green onion."

The most common cured onion is the yellow onion, identified by the yellow color of the dried outer layer. These are pungent raw and flavorful cooked. They can weigh as little as 1 ounce, as much as 8 ounces. These are available all year long.

White onions are milder and smaller. They are marketed at about 2-ounce size. These can be used in all the same ways as yellow onions, but they are most often used whole for glazed onions, creamed onions, and various garnishes.

Bermudas are also white, but they are much larger, sometimes weighing 1 pound each, with a flattened shape. These are mild and especially good raw for salads and sandwiches. They are seasonal, usually marketed in the spring but occasionally found in summer and early fall. Although we do not see them much in our markets, there are also red Bermudas.

Italian red onions, those found in the braids, are mild and sweet but these have the shortest storage life. Usually sold in the spring and early summer.

Spanish onions were once actually imported from Spain; around 1915 they were sold for 5 to 10 cents a pound, which was considered a large price! Today these are raised extensively in the U.S. They were considered mild and sweet, like the Italian red onions, but that is not always so in today's markets—they can be very sharp.

Pearl onions are very small white onions, usually 2 or 3 to an ounce, and no larger than 1-1/2 inches across the fattest part. These are used for pickling and for garnishes, and especially for Gibson cocktails. The greatest disadvantage to using these is peeling them. If you are in a hurry, frozen pearl onions in loose pack can solve the problem; they keep their flavor and texture very well. Recently California growers have been packing yellow and red pearl onions; they are expensive, but make elegant garnishes and accompaniments.

Peeling large onions is not difficult, but working with small ones is a nuisance. Here's how to proceed: Put the onions in a large saucepan, cover them with boiling water, and boil for 2 to 3 minutes for the tiniest specimens, up to 5 minutes for larger ones. Pearl onions do not need to be prepared for this, but with larger white onions (silverskins), especially if you plan to boil them for 5 minutes, it is best to cut a shallow cross in the root end to prevent bursting. Drain them, rinse with cold water or dump into a bowl of ice water, and drain again. Cut off the root ends and pop them out of the skins. Do not boil longer than these few minutes or several layers of peel will be softened and you will lose too much of the onion in peeling.

Do you hate to work with onions because of the odor? Worry no longer. To keep the fumes from affecting eyes and nose, peel onions inside a plastic bag open at both ends. To remove the odor from your hands, wet them with cold water and pour 1 tablespoon table salt into one palm. Rub the salt in your hands as if washing with a cake of soap, then rinse thoroughly in cold water. Wash with soap in warm water. To avoid onion odor on the breath, chew fresh parsley after eating the onions.

If onions are too pungent, here are 2 ways to proceed: Peel them and slice or chop as needed, then soak the pieces in ice water for 15 to 30 minutes. Or try this method: spread chopped or sliced onions on a plate and sprinkle with salt. Let them rest for 15 minutes, or longer, until onions begin to release juices. When ready to proceed, rinse off the salt and juices and pat dry with paper towels.

Onions can be frozen for later use. Peel and chop or mince them, freeze until solid, then pack in small containers; wrap, seal, and label. To have milder chopped onions, pour boiling water over the prepared onions, let them stay for 1 minute, then drain, cool in ice water, and freeze.

Onions are a good source of potassium and have small amounts of other minerals and some vitamins. They are relatively low in calories. An onion of 100 grams (3-1/2 ounces) will provide 38 calories, slightly less when cooked. The same weight of raw scallions provides 45 calories, again slightly less when cooked.

Use onions with a light hand:

Let onion atoms dwell within the bowl,
And, scarce suspected, animate the whole.

"Recipe for Salad Dressing," Sydney Smith

A Note to Cooks

Some of the recipes call for the use of a blender or food processor. If you lack these appliances, do not discard the recipes. Any food can be sliced, chopped or minced with a chef's knife on a chopping board. A mortar and pestle can be used for grating, and there are inexpensive hand-operated utensils for shredding. The best tool for puréeing is the hand-operated food mill, available in several sizes.

Unsalted butter and olive oil were used in testing recipes. If it matters to the recipe, the ingredient list will specify "unsalted butter"; otherwise use what you prefer, but remember to adjust salt. If butter is prohibited, use margarine instead. Any vegetable oil or polyunsaturated oil can be substituted for olive, but the taste will be slightly different.

All recipes use relatively low amounts of salt and very little sugar; if you prefer more or less, adjust to taste. If either is prohibited, simply omit. You may want to adjust flavor with a little lemon juice or an additional pinch of an herb if salt is omitted. If fructose is permitted, use that in place of cane sugar.

■ Ingredients are listed in **bold** type when they are first mentioned in the instructions and thereafter whenever it seems helpful in following the directions.

Onion and Caviar Canapés

preparation time: 40 minutes
cooking time: 2 minutes to
blanch onions, 15 to 20
minutes to cook eggs
makes 64 tiny canapés, about
16 servings

1 pound firm white or oatmeal bread
2 ounces butter, softened
10 to 12 ounces small white onions or large pearl onions, about 24
8 hard-cooked egg yolks
1 cup minced fresh parsley
2 tablespoons grated lemon rind
1/4 to 1/2 cup mayonnaise
3-3/4 ounces Danish lumpfish caviar or salmon caviar

For best results choose onions about 1 inch in diameter.

1. Use a round cutter 1-1/2 inches in diameter, and cut 4 rounds from each slice of **bread.** Allowing 16 slices to the pound, you will have 64 tiny rounds. Use the tiniest amount of **butter** to coat and seal each round, less than 1/8 teaspoon per round. When all are done, cover with wax paper to prevent drying and set in a cool place.

2. Drop **onions** into a pan of boiling water, boil for 2 minutes, then rinse with cold water. Cut off a slice at the root end and pop onions out of their skins. With a sharp knife cut 3 crosswise slices from each onion. Keep 2 rings in each slice and push out the rest. Set the rings on a plate and cover to prevent drying. There should be at least 64 double rings.

3. Mince the rest of the **onions** and the centers of the slices. Push **egg yolks** through a sieve into onions and add **parsley** and **lemon rind.** Mix well. (If you have a food processor, use the steel blade to grate lemon rind and egg yolk and mince onions and parsley all in the same step.) Stir in the smallest amount of **mayonnaise** that will hold ingredients together like a thick spread.

4. Just before serving, spread a thin layer of the **green and gold mixture** on each tiny **round** (about 1/2 teaspoon). Center an **onion ring** on top, and in the center of the ring drop about 1/3 teaspoon of the **caviar.** Serve with cocktails, vodka or Champagne; each canapé makes 1 bite.

5. There will be some of the spread left over; it's good on crackers or other toast rounds.

variation: If caviar is too expensive, fill the centers with tiny amounts of other seafood or even with a mushroom slice.

Onion and Cheese Pastries

preparation time: 20 minutes
cooking time: 1 hour
makes 32 triangles, about 16
servings

1 pound phyllo (fillo) pastry (24 sheets)
2 pounds yellow onions
6 ounces butter
2 tablespoons olive oil
1 teaspoon ground cuminseed
1 cup minced fresh coriander (Chinese parsley)
1/2 pound Edam, Port-Salut or Jarlsberg cheese

If you don't mind buttery pastry bits on the carpets, this makes a delicious snack with drinks; be sure to provide lots of paper napkins.

1. Remove **pastry** from refrigerator, but do not unwrap it; let it reach room temperature. Peel and mince **onions.** Melt the **butter** and set it in a warm place where it will remain liquid.
2. Heat **oil** in a large skillet and add 2 tablespoons of the melted **butter.** Add minced **onions** and cook them over moderate heat, stirring often, until they are very soft and golden; allow at least 30 minutes for this. Toward the end of cooking, mix in the **cuminseed.** Remove from heat and stir in **coriander.** Let onions cool.
3. While onions cook, shred or grate the **cheese.** When onions are cool, stir in the cheese and mix well.
4. Unwrap the **pastry** and spread 1 sheet flat on a pastry board. Brush lightly with **melted butter.** Add a second sheet and brush with butter. Add a third sheet. With a sharp knife cut the pile of sheets lengthwise into 4 narrow strips.
5. Place 1 to 1-1/2 teaspoons of the **onion and cheese mixture** near the top of each strip, then fold over to form a triangle and continue to fold, as if folding the flag, and brushing every second fold with **melted butter.** Fold in the end of each strip to make a neat package. Transfer the triangles to a baking sheet. Brush the tops with a little more butter.
6. Continue to butter and fill the rest of the pastry sheets in piles of 3, until all are done. You may need to use 2 baking sheets for all 32 triangles. Just before serving, bake them in a preheated 375°F. oven for about 30 minutes, until golden and crisp. Serve them while still quite warm.

variation: Use other cheeses for a different taste. Stir in 1/3 cup chopped pimiento for color contrast. If you cannot find coriander in your market, use parsley and add a few drops of lemon juice.

9

Onions Monégasque

preparation time: 15 minutes
cooking time: about 1 hour
makes about 4 cups, 16 hors-
d'oeuvre servings

3 pounds pearl onions or very small silverskins
1-1/2 cups water
1/2 cup white-wine vinegar
3 tablespoons olive oil
3 tablespoons tomato purée
1 teaspoon salt
1 tablespoon granulated sugar
8 parsley sprigs
1 large bay leaf
1 sprig of dried thyme
4 peppercorns
2 whole cloves

These onions are usually served in a shallow ravier as one of the hors-d'oeuvre variés, or simply as one of a selection of three or four served at table. However, they can be used as a relish to accompany meat dishes. They will keep refrigerated for at least a week.

1. Drop **onions** into a pot of boiling water and let them boil for 2 minutes. Drain, rinse with cold water, and drain again. Cut off root ends and pop the onions out of their·skins.
2. In a heavy saucepan combine **water, vinegar, oil, tomato purée, salt** and **sugar.** Stir over low heat until sugar and salt are dissolved and no longer grainy. Separate **parsley leaves** from the **stems.** Put **stems, bay leaf** and **thyme** in a large cheesecloth square. In a mortar crush **peppercorns** and **cloves** and add to the herbs. Tie cheesecloth together, leaving ample room for the herbs and spices to move. Add to the saucepan. Chop the **parsley leaves** and set aside for later.
3. Add **onions** to the saucepan and slowly bring to a boil. Reduce to a bare simmer, partly cover the pan, and let onions cook for almost an hour. They should keep their shape and not separate or fall apart. If they seem to be doing that, remove from heat sooner.
4. Let **onions** cool. Discard cheesecloth bag of **herbs and spices.** Serve onions with some of the cooking liquid, and sprinkle with **chopped parsley.**

variation: If you are in a hurry, make this with frozen pearl onions. They are already peeled; they will need only about 45 minutes of cooking.

Onions and Raisins

eparation time: 10 to 15
minutes
oking time: about 30
minutes
ves 6 as vegetable, 12 as
hors-d'oeuvre

2 pounds pearl onions
1-1/2 ounces butter
2 tablespoons granulated sugar
1 cup moderately sweet white wine
1 cup chicken stock
1 bay leaf
salt (optional)
10 ounces golden raisins
10 fresh mint leaves

This dish can be served as an hors-d'oeuvre with a selection of others, but be sure none of the others is sweet. Or use it as a vegetable accompaniment to poultry or game birds.

1. Drop **onions** into a pot of boiling water and let them boil for 2 minutes. Drain, rinse with cold water, and drain again. Cut off the root ends and pop the onions out of their skins.

2. Melt the **butter** in a saucepan and sauté the **onions,** turning them often, until they are all buttered and beginning to look golden. Sprinkle in the **sugar** and continue to sauté over low heat, shaking the pan, until the onions are lightly browned.

3. Pour in **wine** and **stock,** add **bay leaf,** and simmer **onions** for about 15 minutes, until they are completely tender and the liquid somewhat syrupy. Taste and add **salt** if needed.

4. Stir in the **raisins** and cook over low heat until raisins are plumped up and hot and the syrup a little thicker. Wash and dry **mint leaves** and use as a garnish, either whole or snipped to little slivers.

variation: Instead of raisins use green Thompson seedless grapes, whole, or red Emperor grapes, peeled or not as you prefer, but split and with pits removed.

Shrimps, Onions and Mushrooms

preparation time: about 30
    minutes, plus 2 hours for
    marinating
cooking time: about 25
    minutes
serves 6 as a first course

1 pound medium-size shrimps, about 30
1 tablespoon crab boil or pickling spices
1 bay leaf
sea salt crystals
12 ounces pearl onions
12 ounces button mushrooms
3 lemons
1 teaspoon dry mustard
6 tablespoons light olive oil
6 lettuce leaves (optional)
3 tablespoons minced fresh parsley
2 tablespoons snipped chives

Even though 30 to a pound is called "medium," these are rather small shrimps, so do not overcook them; they should remain juicy and tender to match the vegetables.

1. Peel raw **shrimps** and drop them into a stainless-steel or enamelware saucepan with a tight-fitting lid. Add the **crab boil** or **spices,** the **bay leaf,** and 1 teaspoon **sea salt** crystals. Cover with cold water and bring to a boil. As soon as the water boils, cover the pot and pour off the water. Set the covered pot aside for 8 minutes, then test a small piece of shrimp. As these are small, they should be done; if not, let them stay covered for a few more minutes.

2. Rinse **shrimps** with room temperature water to wash off the bits of spice, then devein them if necessary. To give the appearance of more shrimps, split them lengthwise; however, even whole there should be about 5 shrimps per serving, ample for a first course. Put shrimps in a plastic or pottery bowl.

3. Drop **onions** into a saucepan, cover with boiling water, and boil for 3 minutes. Drain, rinse with cold water, and drain again. Cut off the root ends and pop the onions out of their skins. Return peeled onions to the saucepan.

4. Trim the stems of the **mushrooms** and wipe them with a damp cloth. Do not wash them unless they are very soiled.

5. Grate the **lemon rinds** and measure 1 tablespoon. Any remaining rind can be refrigerated or frozen. Squeeze the **lemons.** Measure 3 tablespoons juice into a small bowl for the dressing.

6. Cover peeled **onions** with water and add 1 tablespoon of the remaining **lemon juice** and 1/2 teaspoon **sea salt** crystals. Bring to a boil and simmer for 5 minutes. Add the **mushrooms** and continue to simmer for 3 more minutes, until both onions and mushrooms are tender. Drain, and add to the shrimps.

7. Measure 1/2 teaspoon **sea salt,** or more to your taste, into the 3 tablespoons **lemon juice,** and add the **mustard.** Stir until salt and mustard are dissolved. Beat in the **olive oil.** Pour the dressing into the **shrimps** and **vegetables,** add the grated **lemon rind,** and mix well.

8. Cover the bowl and let everything marinate in the refrigerator for about 2 hours. Shake or stir the mixture every 20 minutes.

9. Before serving let the mixture warm up for 10 minutes, as it is less flavorful when very cold. Arrange 1 **lettuce leaf** on each salad plate, or omit lettuce if you prefer, and spoon **shrimps** and **vegetables** on top. Combine **parsley** and **chives** and sprinkle over all. Serve with French or Italian bread.

Scallion Omelet-Pancakes (Kuku Sabzi)

aration time: 10 minutes,
plus 30 minutes for batter
to rest
ing time: 10 minutes
s 4 as a first course

4 eggs
3 tablespoons whole-wheat flour
2 tablespoons dried parsley
1 tablespoon dried dill
1 teaspoon salt
15 scallions, no thicker than a pencil
1 onion, 3 ounces
6 tablespoons olive or vegetable oil
1/4 teaspoon ground turmeric
1/8 teaspoon ground coriander
1/8 teaspoon ground cuminseed

This Middle Eastern dish is usually baked in the oven and served with rice. Instead, cook the batter to make tiny pancakes, for an unusual first course.

1. Break **eggs** into a bowl and beat to mix. Stir in **flour, dried herbs** and **salt.** Mix again; set aside for 30 minutes to let starch granules swell.

2. Wash, trim, and mince **scallions.** Peel and mince **onion.**

3. Heat 2 tablespoons **oil** in a large skillet and sauté onion until golden. Stir in **spices** and cook for 2 minutes. Stir **onion-spice mixture** and **scallions** into the **eggs.**

4. Heat 2 more tablespoons **oil** in the same skillet. Drop batter, 2 tablespoons at a time, into the pan to make tiny omelet-pancakes. Cook for about 2 minutes on a side, until browned. Serve warm, at room temperature or cold.

13

Scallions à la Grecque

preparation time: 10 minutes, plus time for cooling
cooking time: about 10 minutes
serves 6

4 bunches of scallions, about 48, none thicker than a pencil
2 cups dry white wine
1/2 cup olive oil
2 tufts of celery leaves
10 parsley stems
1 bay leaf
1 teaspoon sea salt crystals
8 peppercorns
8 coriander berries
1/2 teaspoon cuminseeds
1 teaspoon dried thyme
6 strips of pimiento, tomato or lemon peel
chopped parsley

Serve these with a selection of other hors-d'oeuvre, or as a cold vegetable with summer meals that include aspic dishes, grain salads, cold fish.

1. Wash and trim **scallions.** Use as much of the green leaves as you like, but cut the scallions to the same length.
2. Use a saucepan large enough to hold the scallions. Pour in the **wine** and **olive oil** and add **celery leaves, parsley stems, bay leaf** and **sea salt.** Crush the **spices** and **thyme** in a mortar and tie them in a square of cheesecloth. Add these to the saucepan. Place **scallions** in the pan and add enough **water** to cover them.
3. Bring the liquid to a boil and simmer for about 8 minutes, or until the scallions are done to your taste; try not to let them become limp. Let **scallions** cool in the cooking liquid.
4. Drain cold **scallions** and arrange in 6 bundles on a serving platter. Garnish each bundle with a strip of **pimiento, tomato or lemon peel.** Spoon a little of the cold dressing over the scallions to prevent drying, but they should not be drippy or soupy. Sprinkle with **parsley.** Refrigerate the liquid; it can be used to cook other vegetables.

variation: For a large buffet party, cook equal amounts of celery quarters, fennel quarters, Belgian endive halves and carrot strips, and arrange them and the scallions on shallow platters.

Onion Soup Gratiné

paration time: 15 minutes
oking time: about 45
minutes
ves 6

2 pounds yellow onions
2 ounces butter
1 tablespoon olive oil
6 cups beef stock
salt
6 thick slices of French bread
3 ounces Gruyère cheese
2 ounces Parmesan cheese

This soup is what most people expect when they ask for "French Onion Soup" but it is only one of many onion soups invented by French cooks. An excellent supper dish, actually better for that meal than as the start of a more formal dinner.

1. Peel and slice **onions.** Melt **butter** in a deep saucepan, add **oil,** and gently cook onions, turning them often with a wooden spoon, until golden all through but not at all browned.
2. Pour in the **stock,** bring to a boil, then simmer for 20 minutes, until **onions** start to melt in the stock. Taste. If you have used unsalted butter and unsalted stock, you may want to add a little **salt,** but remember the cheese will be salty.
3. While the soup is cooking, dry the **bread slices** in a slow oven. Grate both **cheeses** and mix together. Put 1 slice of **bread** in each of 6 flameproof earthenware soup pots, and sprinkle with half of the **cheese.** Pour in **hot soup** to fill the pots; the bread will come floating to the top. Sprinkle with the rest of the **cheese.**
4. Slide the filled soup pots under the broiler and let them stay there just long enough to make the cheese bubble. Serve without delay.

variation: Some cooks prefer to strain out the onions before adding soup to the earthenware pots. It is good either way.

15

Onion Soup with Wine

preparation time: 15 minutes
cooking time: about 50
    minutes
serves 6

2 pounds yellow onions
2-1/2 ounces butter
1 tablespoon olive oil
4 cups chicken stock
2 cups dry white wine
salt and white pepper
1 bunch of scallions, about 12

1. Peel and slice **onions.** Melt 2 ounces of the **butter** in a deep saucepan, add **oil,** and gently cook **onions,** turning them often with a wooden spoon, until golden all through but not at all browned.

2. Pour in **stock** and **wine,** bring to a boil, then simmer for 30 minutes, until **onions** are almost dissolved in the stock. Taste, and add **salt** as necessary and a pinch or two of **white pepper.**

3. Purée the soup, part at a time, in a blender or food processor, or put through a food mill. Return to the saucepan and reheat.

4. Meanwhile, wash and trim **scallions.** Keep about 2 inches of the green part (use the rest for flavoring stock). Chop scallions. Melt remaining **butter** in a small skillet and sauté scallions until tender.

5. Serve the soup in a tureen, or in individual bowls, sprinkled with the scallions. Toasted English muffins and toasted pita bread are good accompaniments for this soup.

Cream of Onion Soup

Preparation time: 15 minutes
Cooking time: about 50
minutes
Serves 6

2 pounds white onions
2 ounces butter
1 tablespoon olive oil
1 teaspoon salt
2 cups chicken stock
2 cups water
juice of 1 lemon
2 eggs
2 cups light cream
3 tablespoons snipped chives

This is a delicate onion soup, an excellent choice for a party luncheon, and also good invalid food for anyone who can eat onions.

1. Peel and chop the **onions.** Melt **butter** in a deep saucepan, add **oil,** and gently cook **onions,** turning them often, until they are translucent. Sprinkle with **salt.**

2. Pour in **stock, water** and **lemon juice,** and bring to a boil. Simmer for 30 minutes.

3. Beat **eggs** and **cream** together in a bowl. Pour in about 1 cup of the **hot soup,** whisking to blend well. Then pour the egg mixture into the rest of the soup, whisking all the while.

4. Bring the **soup** to serving temperature, but do not let it boil. Serve in a tureen or in cream-soup bowls, and sprinkle with **chives.**

Swiss Onion Soup

preparation time: 15 minutes
cooking time: about 1 hour
serves 6

1-1/2 pounds yellow onions
4 ounces butter
1 pound small potatoes
4 cups water
salt
4 ounces Emmental cheese

1. Peel and slice **onions.** Melt **butter** in a heavy 2-quart saucepan and in it sauté **onions,** turning them over now and then, until tender. Do not brown them.
2. Peel **potatoes,** cover with the **water,** and add a little **salt.** Bring to a boil and simmer until potatoes are ready to fall apart. Put **potatoes** and **water** through a food mill into the pan of onions.
3. Simmer the mixture, stirring often, for 30 to 40 minutes. Grate the **cheese** into a tureen and pour in the **soup.** Stir to blend and serve at once, before cheese gets rubbery.

variation: Use 2 cups water for potatoes. Add 2 cups Swiss white wine to the mixture of onions and potatoes at the end of Step 2.

Steam-Baked Onions

preparation time: 5 minutes
cooking time: 1-1/2 to 2 hours
serves 6

6 large yellow onions, each about 6 ounces
1-1/2 to 2 cups water
salt and pepper
3 ounces butter

1. Do not peel the **onions.** Put onions in a baking dish large enough to hold them in a single layer. Pour in enough of the **water** to have about 1 inch in the dish. Cover the dish. Bake in a 300°F. oven for 1-1/2 to 2 hours, until onions feel soft.
2. Cut onions open at the stem end and pull back the peel. When you reach the root end, cut it off. Cut each onion from stem to blossom end and spread the halves open. Sprinkle with **salt** and **pepper.** Divide **butter** into 6 thick pats and drop on the onions.
3. Or, if this is an informal meal, serve **onions** in the peel and let each person peel his own. Delicious with mashed potatoes and sausages, steak and hamburgers.

Glazed Onions

paration time: 10 minutes
king time: 20 to 30 minutes
es 6

1-1/2 pounds small white onions (silverskins)
2 ounces butter
3 tablespoons sugar
1 cup chicken stock, hot

1. Cut off **onion** roots and make a cross in each root end. Cover with boiling water and simmer for about 5 minutes. Drain and rinse. As soon as onions are cool enough to handle, peel them.

2. Melt **butter** in skillet and add peeled onions. Sauté them, turning often, until they begin to look golden. Sprinkle **sugar** over **onions** and turn them over.

3. Pour in **stock,** and simmer until liquid is reduced to a sticky glaze and **onions** are coated with a sort of caramel. Serve as a vegetable, or add to stews, where the caramel will add color and flavor to the meat.

variations: Add blanched white turnips and carrots, both cut into rounds with a melon-ball cutter, to the onions in Step 2 for an excellent mixture, especially for stews.

Veal or beef stock can be used if it is more compatible with the meat to be used. Vegetable stock is also good. Brown sugar or honey can be used in place of white sugar.

19

Creamed Onions

preparation time: 15 minutes
cooking time: 20 to 25 minutes
serves 6 to 8

2 pounds white onions (silverskins)
2 cups chicken stock, or half stock, half water
salt (optional)
1 ounce butter
2 tablespoons all-purpose flour
1 cup light cream
paprika or chopped parsley

1. Choose **onions** all the same size. Cut a tiny cross in the root end of each one and drop them into a large pot. Pour in boiling water to cover and let **onions** boil for about 3 minutes. Drain, rinse with cold water, and drain again. With a sharp knife cut off the root ends and pop the onions out of their skins.
2. Drop **onions** into a saucepan and add **stock,** or **stock and water.** If stock is unsalted, add a scant 1 teaspoon **salt.** Bring to a simmer and cook very gently until onions are tender, 10 to 15 minutes.
3. Melt **butter** in a separate saucepan. Off the heat stir in the **flour,** then over low heat cook for a few minutes; add **cream,** stirring with a whisk all the while to blend well. The sauce will become rather thick, but onions will thin it.
4. With a skimmer transfer **onions** to **cream sauce** and mix. If the sauce is too thick, add a little of the cooking stock, a few tablespoons at a time. (Remaining cooking stock can be used for soup.) If there is a delay in serving, keep the onions hot over hot water. Sprinkle with **paprika** or **parsley** just before serving.

variations: To give a different flavor, use half sweet cream and half sour cream in the sauce. Grated Parmesan cheese can be added to the sauce, or cheese and crumbs can be sprinkled on top to give a gratin topping.
For an unusual service, spoon onions into pastry boats or toasted croustades. To use these onions as a garnish, spoon about 3 onions and some of the sauce into hollowed-out small tomatoes or artichoke bottoms; arrange them around a roast or a broiled steak.

Onions with Grated Cheese

preparation time: 15 minutes
cooking time: about 30
minutes
serves 6

1-1/2 pounds Spanish onions or yellow onions
1-1/2 ounces butter
2 tablespoons olive oil
1/2 cup chicken stock
1/2 cup white Chianti wine or other flavorful Italian wine
3 ounces Locatelli Romano cheese
3 tablespoons minced flat-leaf parsley

1. Peel and slice **onions.** Melt **butter** in a skillet, add **oil,** and sauté onions until translucent and tender.
2. Pour in **stock** and **wine** and gently simmer for about 10 minutes, until liquid is reduced to a small amount of glaze. Remove skillet from direct heat.
3. Meanwhile grate the **cheese.** Just before serving, sprinkle **cheese** over the **onions.** Cover the skillet and let the pan remain in a warm place until cheese starts to melt.
4. Sprinkle with **parsley** and serve at once. Excellent with veal scallops and pork tenderloin.

A French Garnish

preparation time: 15 to 20
minutes
cooking time: 20 to 30 minutes
serves 6 to 8

1 pound pearl onions
1 pound button mushrooms
1 ounce butter
juice of 1 lemon
1-1/2 cups veal stock
4 ounces medium-dry white wine or Madeira
3 tablespoons tomato purée
salt and pepper
minced parsley

In French cuisine a garnish is not a limp parsley sprig or tired lemon slice, but an accompaniment, usually vegetable, to the main ingredient—the meat, poultry, or fish. The tiny onions give the French appearance. This mixture is especially suitable for poultry.

1. Cover unpeeled **onions** with boiling water and simmer for 3 minutes. Drain, cool, and peel onions. Trim mushroom stems and wipe **mushrooms** with a damp cloth.
2. Melt **butter** in a deep saucepan and add **onions** and **mushrooms.** Sauté, turning often with a wooden spoon, until onions begin to look golden and mushrooms release a lot of liquid.
3. Pour in **lemon juice, stock, wine** and **tomato purée.** Mix gently. Simmer, uncovered, until liquid is reduced to a sauce texture and vegetables are tender. Season with **salt and pepper.**
4. When serving the garnish, use just enough of the sauce to moisten the mixture. Sprinkle with **parsley.**

variations: If you lack fresh pearl onions, use frozen onions, an excellent substitute; they will be already peeled. However, do not use frozen mushrooms as the flavor is too different.
Veal stock is best as it has gelatin in it, but use the stock that matches your dish if you prefer; chicken or beef can be used. The stock should not quite cover the vegetables. Use only as much of 1-1/2 cups as you need.

Onions and Chestnuts

:paration time: 20 minutes
oking time: 40 to 50 minutes
ves 6 to 8

1 pound fresh chestnuts in shells
oil
2 cups chicken stock
salt
1 large bay leaf
1-1/2 pounds small white onions (silverskins)
2 ounces butter
cayenne pepper
1/4 cup chopped parsley

1. Cut a cross in the rounded side of the shell of each **chestnut** and place them in a single layer on an oiled baking sheet. Roast them in a preheated 350°F. oven for about 20 minutes, until the shells curl away from the cuts. Shake the pan now and then.

2. As soon as **chestnuts** are cool enough to handle, remove the shells and as much of the peel as possible. Drop them into a saucepan of boiling water and boil them for about 5 minutes. Lift out a few at a time and remove all the inner peel. These 2 steps can be done a day ahead.

3. Put peeled **chestnuts** in a clean saucepan and add the **stock.** If it is unsalted, add 1/2 teaspoon **salt.** Also drop in the **bay leaf.** Bring to a simmer and cook until chestnuts are quite tender. Drain them, but reserve the remaining stock.

4. Cut off **onion** roots and make a cross in each root end. Cover with boiling water and simmer for about 5 minutes. Drain and rinse. As soon as onions are cool enough to handle, peel them.

5. Melt **butter** in a saucepan and add peeled **onions.** Sauté, turning them often, until they begin to color. Stir in the cooked **chestnuts** and pour in about 1 cup of the reserved **stock.** Sprinkle in a dash of **cayenne.**

6. Bring **stock** to a simmer and cook for 5 minutes, until vegetables are tender and most of the liquid absorbed. Sprinkle with **parsley.** Serve with poultry or rabbit dishes.

variation: In a hurry, use frozen pearl onions and dried chestnuts. The day before, pour boiling water over the chestnuts to cover them by 3 inches. Next day, drain and scrape off any remaining peel. Go on with Step 3. Defrost the onions and proceed from Step 5.

23

Onions and Almonds in Wine Sauce

preparation time: 10 to 15 minutes
cooking time: about 1 hour
serves 6

2 pounds small white onions (silverskins)
3 ounces butter
8 ounces blanched almonds
2 eggs
1 cup medium-dry white wine or sherry
1/2 cup chicken stock
salt and white pepper
1/2 cup soft fresh bread crumbs

A party dish, delicious as accompaniment to poultry, game or veal. Serve wild rice, brown rice or cracked wheat for perfect flavor contrast.

1. Drop **onions** into a pot of boiling water and let them boil for 2 minutes. Drain, rinse with cold water, and drain again. Cut off the root ends and pop the onions out of their skins.
2. Melt half of the **butter** in a skillet and in it sauté the whole **almonds** until delicately browned; do not overcook. Use a slotted spoon to transfer almonds to a 4-cup casserole. Add **onions** to skillet and sauté them briefly until barely golden. Add to almonds. Set skillet aside. Preheat oven to 350°F.
3. In a bowl beat **eggs** with **wine** and **stock** until well mixed. Season with **salt** and a little **white pepper** to taste. Pour into the casserole. Partly cover casserole, and bake for 30 minutes.
4. Meanwhile, melt remaining **butter** in the skillet and stir in the **bread crumbs** until they are well buttered. Remove cover from casserole. Spread crumbs on top of **onions** and **almonds** and bake uncovered for 20 to 30 minutes longer, until crumbs are browned and crispy and onions tender.

Curried Onions and Fenugreek Sprouts

paration time: 10 minutes
king time: 15 to 20 minutes
es 4

1-1/4 to 1-1/2 cups fenugreek sprouts
salt
1 pound small white onions (silverskins)
1 yellow onion, 2 ounces
2 tablespoons vegetable oil
1 teaspoon curry powder
2 tablespoons chicken stock or water
2 tablespoons dried currants

1. Pour boiling water over the **sprouts,** add 1/2 teaspoon **salt,** and return to the boil. Boil for 2 minutes, then drain and rinse with cold water; drain again and set aside.

2. Trim roots from **white onions,** and cut a cross in the root end of each one. Sprinkle onions with 1 teaspoon **salt,** cover with boiling water, and return to a simmer for 10 minutes. Drain onions, rinse with cold water, and peel them.

3. Peel and chop the **yellow onion.** Heat the **vegetable oil** in a large skillet and sauté chopped **onion** until translucent. Add **curry powder** and cook and stir until curry powder, oil and onion are completely mixed.

4. Add the peeled whole **onions** and sauté for a few minutes. Add drained **fenugreek sprouts,** stir, then pour in the **stock** or **water.** Cover the skillet and cook over low heat until onions are tender.

5. Stir in the **currants** and heat. Add a little more **salt** if needed. Serve with poultry or lamb. Or if you use water instead of stock, serve as a vegetarian dish with rice and almonds. Garnish with fresh coriander if you serve it with rice.

variations: Everything can be adjusted to taste. Use more or less curry powder. Use other sprouts, although fenugreek adds the best flavor for curry. Augment the dish with 1 pound zucchini, diced, added with the whole onions.

To get this amount of sprouts, start with 1.5 ounces of seeds. Harvest them after 3 days; if they grow larger, they become bitter.

Onions and Celery Avgolemono

preparation time: 15 minutes
cooking time: about 30
minutes
serves 6 to 8

1-1/2 pounds small white onions (silverskins)
1 yellow onion, 4 ounces
1 pound tender celery ribs
1 ounce butter
1 tablespoon olive oil
1-1/2 cups chicken stock
salt and white pepper
1/4 teaspoon crumbled dried rosemary
2 eggs
juice of 1 lemon
1/4 cup minced fresh coriander or fresh parsley

Avgolemono (egg and lemon) is a favorite Greek sauce. It can be used on poultry, fish and other vegetables, but we think it is especially good with onions and celery.

1. Cut a tiny cross at the root end of the **white onions** and drop them into a saucepan of boiling water. Boil for 3 minutes, then drain, rinse with cold water, and drain again. Cut off the root ends and pop each onion out of its skin. Set them aside.
2. Peel and chop the **yellow onion.** Wash and dry **celery** and cut across into 3/4-inch pieces, including any tender leaves.
3. Melt **butter** in a saucepan and add the **oil.** Sauté the chopped **yellow onion** until golden. Add the whole **white onions** and stir over heat for 2 minutes, until they begin to show a little color. Add the **celery.**
4. Pour in the **stock.** Add 1/2 teaspoon **salt,** 2 pinches of **white pepper** and the **rosemary.** Stir to mix well, then bring to a simmer and cook uncovered, stirring occasionally, until **celery** and **white onions** are tender.
5. Break **eggs** into a bowl and add the **lemon juice.** Beat with a rotary beater until well mixed. Pour off the stock from the vegetables and measure 1/2 cup. With a whisk beat the **eggs** while pouring in the hot 1/2 cup **stock.** At once pour the egg mixture into the **vegetables** and mix gently but thoroughly. Set the saucepan on an asbestos pad over heat and let it rest for 1 to 2 minutes, until the sauce thickens lightly.
6. Sprinkle with **coriander** or **parsley,** mix again, and serve at once. Good with baked fish and steamed cracked wheat, or with poultry and rice, or with Greek lamb dishes.

Al McClane's Charcoal-Cooked Vegetables

eparation time: 15 minutes,
plus time to build a fire
oking time: about 1 hour
ves 6 or 12

6 whole onions, about 4 ounces each
6 tomatoes, about 6 ounces each
6 green peppers, about 6 ounces each
12 mushrooms
1/2 cup garlic butter, melted
celery salt
black pepper
minced fresh parsley
minced fresh tarragon

These vegetables are delicious with rice and charcoal-cooked beef, lamb and game (deer, elk, moose). Vegetables are full of flavor, slightly smoky from hickory chips. Onions are sweet and crunchy and there are no "burps."

1. Make a hot charcoal fire in a covered barbecue. Throw a handful of wet hickory chips on the coals. Place the **unpeeled onions** on the grill and cook with the lid down for 30 to 40 minutes. Use tongs to roll onions around to cook evenly. The outer skin will turn black. Remove onions from the fire.
2. While onions cook, wash and dry **tomatoes** and cut crosswise into halves. Trim **green peppers,** discarding stems, ribs and seeds, and quarter the peppers. Trim mushroom stems and wipe **mushrooms** with a damp cloth.
3. Add more hickory chips to the fire. Arrange **tomato halves, pepper quarters** and **mushrooms** on the grill and cook for 15 to 20 minutes. Turn **tomatoes** with tongs so both round sides and cut sides are cooked; skin will crack, turn golden, and blister. Turn **pepper** pieces over once or twice; peppers will blister and show black patches.
4. Hold each **onion** with a paper towel and press down and inward; onions will pop out of their skins. Cut onions crosswise into halves and place in a shallow roasting pan. Peel skin off **peppers** and add to onions, along with **tomatoes** and **mushrooms.**
5. Drizzle **garlic butter** over vegetables and sprinkle with **seasoning** and **herbs** to taste. Keep warm in a low oven until serving time. All the juices will marry with the butter.
6. Mound cooked rice on a large serving platter and place meat pieces on top. Arrange the **vegetables** around the rice, and pour the butter and juices over the meat. Sprinkle with more **parsley.**

Onions and Peanuts

preparation time: about 10
minutes
cooking time: about 30
minutes
serves 6

2 pounds white onions (silverskins)
1/2 teaspoon salt
1 ounce unsalted butter
1 cup chicken stock
1/2 cup salted peanuts

This Virginia speciality is an old favorite in the South. The contrast of textures gives this dish a special taste.

1. Drop **onions** into a large saucepan of boiling water and boil for 3 minutes. Drain, rinse in cold water, and drain again. Cut off the root ends and pop onions out of their skins.

2. Return **onions** to the saucepan, add the **salt** and water to cover, and simmer the onions until tender but not mushy. Drain. These steps can be done a day ahead.

3. Melt **butter** in a skillet and add the cooked **onions.** Stir them or shake the pan until all the onions are coated with butter. Pour in the **stock** and cook over low heat, stirring the onions or shaking the pan, until the stock is reduced by half.

4. Chop the **peanuts** and add them to the **onions.** Cook just long enough to heat everything well, and spoon about 2 tablespoons reduced **stock** over each serving.

Scallions with Cheese Sauce

paration time: 10 minutes
oking time: 20 to 25 minutes
ves 4

32 scallions, as thick as a pencil
1 ounce butter
2 tablespoons all-purpose flour
3/4 cup chicken stock
3/4 cup light cream
1/4 teaspoon black pepper
2 teaspoons prepared Dijon mustard
3 ounces Gruyère cheese
1/4 cup fine dry bread crumbs

1. Wash and trim **scallions.** Leave most of the green leaves on them, but cut them all to the same length. Set them in a steamer over water and steam for about 5 minutes, or until tender to your taste.

2. Melt **butter** in a saucepan, stir in **flour,** then pour in both **stock** and **cream** and cook over low heat, stirring, until the mixture thickens slightly. Sprinkle in the **pepper** and stir in **mustard.**

3. Grate the **cheese** and mix about a third of it with the **bread crumbs.** Stir remaining **cheese** into the **sauce;** it will melt in the heat of the sauce.

4. Divide **scallions** among 4 individual oval gratin dishes. Pour about 6 tablespoons of the **sauce** over each bundle of scallions. Sprinkle the **crumb and cheese mixture** over the sauced scallions. Slide under the broiler until the scallions are hot and the crumb topping golden. Serve as a first course, or with plain chicken or chops.

variation: Set scallions on buttered toast for a more substantial dish.

French-Fried Onion Rings

preparation time: about 40 minutes
cooking time: about 20 minutes
serves 8 or more

2 pounds large Spanish onions
1 cup all-purpose flour
1/2 teaspoon salt
1/2 teaspoon curry powder
1 egg, separated
1 cup flat beer
3 cups vegetable oil

1. Peel **onions** and cut into crosswise slices about 1/2 inch thick. Do not use the ends, but set them aside for another use. Separate slices into rings. Fill a large bowl with ice cubes, add onion rings, and pour in water to cover them. Let them soak in the ice water for 30 minutes or longer.

2. Make batter. Mix **flour, salt** and **curry powder** in a bowl. Beat **egg yolk** and **beer** together, and stir into the flour mixture. Beat until smooth, then refrigerate for 30 minutes.

3. Beat **egg white** with a whisk, then whisk it into the **batter.** Drain **onion rings** and dry them thoroughly in paper towels.

4. Heat **oil** in a deep-fryer or a wok to 380°F. Dip **onion rings** into the **batter,** remove and let them drain for a second. Lower the frying basket into hot oil, then fill it with a layer of **batter-dipped pieces** and fry until golden and puffed. Turn rings over to brown evenly. When tender, lift out to a baking sheet lined with paper towels, and keep warm in a low oven until all rings are fried. Be sure the oil returns to 380°F. before starting each new batch.

5. Sprinkle **onion rings** with **salt** only when ready to serve them. Serve as a topping on vegetable casseroles, as a garnish for steaks and hamburgers, or as a vegetable accompaniment to picnic foods.

Rice-Stuffed Onions

paration time: 15 minutes
king time: about 1-1/2
      hours
es 4

2 Bermuda onions, about 1 pound each
salt
1/2 cup brown rice
juice of 1/2 lemon
olive oil
2 ounces butter
2 ounces slivered blanched almonds
2 ounces slivered pimientos

These onions are a perfect mate for baked poultry, but good also with roast lamb or chops. They are a little fussy to make, but you will like the results. For a buffet, just multiply everything; in one dish you will have starch and vegetable.

1. Carefully halve **onions** crosswise, making even pieces, and peel them. Arrange them in a steamer basket over 1-1/2 cups water. Sprinkle them lightly with **salt.** Steam for about 20 minutes, until about half done. Discard water and let onions cool.
2. Put **rice** in a saucepan with a tight-fitting cover. Add 1-1/2 cups **cold water,** the **lemon juice,** a few drops of **oil,** and 1/2 teaspoon **salt.** Bring to a boil, cover, then reduce to a simmer and cook for about 20 minutes, until rice is tender but not mushy; the pan should not be dry.
3. When **onions** are cool enough to handle, carefully scoop out the centers, leaving about 3 layers of shell. Oil a shallow baking dish and arrange the shells in it.
4. Chop scooped-out **centers** roughly. Melt 1 ounce of the **butter** in a skillet and sauté the **chopped onion** until pieces begin to show the faintest edge of brown. Turn the whole mixture into a food processor fitted with the steel blade, or into a blender, and chop to small pieces. Preheat oven to 375°F.
5. Melt remaining **butter** in the skillet and sauté **almonds** until lightly browned. Return **onions** to the pan, mix, then stir in **pimientos** and **rice.** Mix well. Spoon the filling into the **onion shells,** mounding it up in the middle.
6. Cover dish with a sheet of foil and bake **onions** for about 45 minutes. Use a large shallow spoon or pancake turner to transfer them to a serving dish or individual plates.

Onions Stuffed with Chicken Livers

preparation time: 30 minutes
cooking time: about 1-1/2
hours
serves 6

6 large red onions, each 8 to 10 ounces
12 ounces chicken livers
2 tablespoons olive oil
3 tablespoons minced parsley
1/4 teaspoon ground cuminseed
salt and pepper
1 cup dry red wine
1 cup soft fresh bread crumbs
2 slices bacon

Serve these for an unusual first course, accompanied with toast strips, or for a small luncheon, accompanied with a green salad.

1. Peel the **onions;** remove roots but just barely trim the base as it is needed to hold onions together. Cut a slice across the stem end, making a flat surface at least 2-1/2 inches across. Pierce each **onion** twice with a thin skewer. Set them in a steamer and steam over 1-1/2 cups water for 20 to 30 minutes, until they are nearly done. Let them drain and cool. Discard the water.
2. Put **livers** in a bowl and pour boiling water over them. When water reaches room temperature, drain livers. Trim and cut into small chunks.
3. Use a melon-ball scoop or a grapefruit knife to scoop out the insides of the **onions.** Leave at least 3 layers for the shell and try not to damage it. Chop the scooped-out pieces.
4. Heat **oil** in a skillet and sauté **chopped onion** until it is very soft. Add **liver pieces** and cook until they are browned. Stir in **parsley** and **cuminseed** and season with **salt** and **pepper** to taste. Pour in the **wine** and let the mixture simmer until wine is reduced by half. Preheat oven to 350°F.
5. Stir in enough **bread crumbs** to make a soft but still moist mixture. Sprinkle **onion shells** with **salt** and stuff them with the **liver mixture.** (If there is any left over, bake it in a small custard dish.)
6. Sauté the **bacon** until half cooked. Drain the slices, then cut each one into 3 pieces. Place 1 piece on top of each **onion,** covering the stuffing. Set **onions** in a dish that just holds them, or balance them on a ring of foil so they do not tip over. Cover the pan.
7. Bake the **onions** for 20 minutes, then uncover the pan and continue to bake for 20 to 30 minutes until onions are tender and **bacon** crisp.

variation: If you don't use bacon, brush the onions with melted butter or oil when you uncover them, to prevent drying.

Onion and Cheese Charlotte

Preparation time: 20 minutes
Cooking time: 1 hour and 45 minutes
Serves 4 as main course, 6 as accompaniment

3 pounds Spanish or yellow onions
6 ounces butter
1 large lemon
1 pound unsliced firm white bread
1 ounce Parmesan cheese
8 ounces whole-milk mozzarella cheese
2 teaspoons cornstarch
1 cup milk or light cream
salt and pepper
1 teaspoon grated mace
1/2 cup chopped parsley

This upside-down pudding makes a good vegetarian main dish, accompanied by a green salad, but it can also be served with veal or lamb.

1. Peel **onions** and cut into chunks. Cover with boiling water and simmer until half done. Drain well.
2. Melt 3 ounces of the **butter** in a large skillet and add drained **onions.** Cook over low heat, stirring often, for about 40 minutes, until onions are "melted." Grate **lemon rind** into the onions and squeeze the **lemon juice** into them. Preheat oven to 375°F.
3. Meanwhile, cut the **bread** into thick slices, remove crusts, and cut slices to line exactly the sides of a 1-quart charlotte mold, with some pieces to fit the round bottom. Use a little of the **butter** to coat the inside of the mold. Grate **Parmesan cheese** and sprinkle it evenly over the butter. Save any unused cheese for the filling
4. Melt remaining **butter** and sauté the pieces of **bread** until just golden. Carefully arrange them in the mold. Shred **mozzarella cheese.**
5. When **onions** are done, purée them in a food processor fitted with the steel blade, or push them through a food mill. Mix **cornstarch** into the **cold milk** and stir it into the **onion purée.** Cook over low heat until the mixture is very thick. Season with **salt** and **pepper** and stir in **mace.** Remove from heat and stir in shredded **mozzarella** and any remaining **Parmesan.** Let the mixture cool for a few minutes.
6. Fill the lined mold with the **purée,** cover with a sheet of foil, and bake for about 45 minutes. The bread should be toasted and the filling very hot. Use a thin flexible knife to release the pudding from the mold. Turn out on a round platter. Sprinkle a border of **parsley** around the base.

Eggs in Ramekins Soubise

preparation time: 10 minutes
cooking time: about 15
      minutes, plus time to
      make Purée Soubise
serves 6

3 cups Purée Soubise (see Index)
1 ounce butter
6 eggs
salt
6 tablespoons meat glaze or tomato purée
2 tablespoons minced parsley

The ramekins (or cocottes) used in this recipe hold 1 cup; if you want a more substantial dish for a luncheon or supper main dish, use larger ramekins that hold 1-1/2 cups and cook 2 eggs per serving.

1. Make the **Purée Soubise.** Use 1 teaspoon **butter** to coat the inside of each ramekin. Put about 1/2 cup of the **purée** in each one, patting it up the sides as much as possible. Preheat oven to 350°F.

2. Break an **egg** into each ramekin. Sprinkle lightly with **salt.** Set ramekins in a large flat saucepan or baking dish and pour in boiling water up to 1/2 inch from the top of the ramekins. Cover the pan. Slide the pan into the oven and bake for about 15 minutes, until the **whites** are just set and the **yolks** are still shiny and soft.

3. Use jar tongs or potholders to lift out the ramekins and dry them. Spoon 1 tablespoon of the **meat glaze** or **tomato purée** around each yolk to make a ribbon. Sprinkle with 1 teaspoon **parsley.** Serve without delay.

Onion Omelet

eparation time: 5 minutes
ooking time: about 20
minutes
rves 1 or 2

1 onion, about 4 ounces
3 flat anchovy fillets
1-1/2 ounces unsalted butter
1 tablespoon olive oil
3 eggs
1-1/2 tablespoons water
2 strips of pimiento

1. Peel and mince the **onion.** Pat **anchovy fillets** with paper towels to remove most of the oil. With scissors cut each fillet into small pieces.
2. Melt 1/2 ounce **butter** in a small saucepan. Add **oil.** Drop in **anchovy pieces** and **minced onion,** and sauté over low heat, stirring often, until anchovies are practically "melted" and onions very soft and tender.
3. Meanwhile break **eggs** into a bowl, add **water,** and beat well. Melt remaining **butter** in a small omelet pan. When it is sizzling, pour in eggs and cook over brisk heat, stirring with a fork, until the omelet is cooked to the point that suits you.
4. Spoon **onion and anchovy mixture** across the middle of the omelet, fold one side over, then turn the **omelet** out on a hot plate, making a triple fold. Drape **pimiento strips** over and serve at once.

Onion Quiche

preparation time: 20 minutes, plus 1 hour for chilling pastry
cooking time: 1 hour and 20 minutes
serves 8 to 10

1 pound short-crust pastry with whole egg
3 tablespoons olive or vegetable oil
2 pounds yellow onions
2 ounces butter
1 teaspoon salt
1/2 teaspoon ground cuminseed
1/4 teaspoon ground coriander
1 cup light cream
3 eggs
1/4 cup minced fresh parsley

In Alsace this tart is called Zewelwai; in Switzerland it is Zwiebelwähe; in France it is Tarte à l'Oignon.

1. Make the **pastry** and chill it in refrigerator for 1 hour. Use 1 tablespoon of the **oil** to coat a 10-inch pottery quiche dish. Roll out **pastry** to a thin sheet and fit it into the dish. Crimp the edges. Let pastry rest in a cold place while making the filling.
2. Peel and slice **onions.** Heat remaining **oil** and the **butter** in a large skillet. Put **onions** in the skillet, cover, and cook over very low heat for 30 to 45 minutes, until onions are almost "melted." Preheat oven to 400°F.
3. Stir **salt** and **spices** into **cream.** Add **eggs** and beat well. Mix in **parsley.**
4. When **onions** are cooked, layer them in the chilled pastry. Slowly pour in the **custard mixture;** if necessary lift onions now and then to distribute custard. Cover the dish with a sheet of foil.
5. Bake in the 400°F. oven for about 15 minutes. Reduce temperature to 375°F., uncover the quiche, and bake for 15 to 20 minutes longer, until custard is firm but still creamy. Serve as a luncheon or supper dish, or cut into small wedges or squares for first course.

variations: Layer about 4 ounces of smoked salmon, cut into thin slivers, among the onions. Or crumble 2 to 3 ounces blue cheese in the onions. In either case adjust the salt to compensate for the salty fish or cheese.

   For party service, bake in individual tart pans. Or use a square baking dish to make serving easy.

Onion and Olive Tart Provençale

paration time: 20 minutes,
plus time for raising pastry
or chilling it
king time: about 1 hour
es 8 to 10

1 pound short-crust or yeast pastry
2 pounds yellow onions
olive oil
salt and pepper
1 cup pitted black olives
2 ounces whole-milk mozzarella cheese, or other soft white cheese of
    delicate taste
12 flat anchovy fillets

1. Make the **pastry.** If it is short-crust, chill it for 1 hour. If it is yeast pastry, let
it rise for 1 hour or longer, until doubled in bulk. Roll out the **pastry** to a sheet
as thin as possible and fit it into an oiled 10-inch tart pan or pottery quiche
dish. Crimp the edges and set in a cold place or the refrigerator to rest.
2. Peel and slice **onions.** Heat 3 tablespoons **oil** in a heavy skillet. Add
onions, cover, and cook over low heat until onions are tender and golden.
Sprinkle with **salt** (not too much) and some **pepper.** Preheat oven to 400°F.
3. Chop **olives.** Shred the **cheese.** Pat **anchovy fillets** to get rid of excess oil.
Spread the cheese in the pastry; it should make a thin layer only. Spread
onions in an even layer on top of the cheese. Sprinkle **olives** over the top
and arrange **anchovies** in a pattern over all.
4. Bake the tart for about 20 minutes. Reduce temperature to 350°F. and
continue to bake the tart until **pastry** is crisp and brown, 15 to 25 minutes
longer. Serve as a luncheon dish or as a first course.

variation: Omit anchovies and decorate the top with about 1 cup fresh
tomato purée. Sprinkle with parsley at serving time.

Onion Cheese Bake

preparation time: 20 minutes
cooking time: about 1-1/4
hours
serves 4 as a main course, 6 as
accompaniment

2 pounds yellow onions
2 ounces unsalted butter
1 tablespoon olive oil
6 ounces firm bread
8 ounces Edam or Gouda cheese
1/2 teaspoon cuminseeds, crushed
Tabasco

1. Peel and chop **onions.** Use some of the **butter** to coat the inside of a 6-cup baking dish and cover (or a sheet of foil if there is no cover). Melt the rest of the **butter** in a large skillet, add the **oil,** and sauté **onions** over low heat, stirring often, until onions are soft and golden; allow at least 30 minutes for this.

2. While onions are slowly "melting," cut the **bread** into 1-inch cubes. Shred the **cheese;** if you shred with a food processor, the cheese should be very cold for best results. Preheat oven to 350°F.

3. Sprinkle a layer of **bread cubes** (about a third of the cubes) in the buttered dish. Cover with half of the **onions** and sprinkle with half of the **cuminseeds** and a few drops of **Tabasco.** Add half of the **shredded cheese.** Continue with another layer of bread cubes, onions, cuminseeds, Tabasco and cheese. Finish with the rest of the bread cubes.

4. Cover, and bake for 30 minutes. Uncover, and bake for 10 to 15 minutes longer, until the **bread cubes** around the edges are beginning to brown. Serve with baked or broiled tomatoes.

variations: For a more nutritious vegetarian main dish, use a 2-quart dish and add 1 cup slivered almonds.

For an onion-cheese custard, mix 2 eggs and 1 cup light cream and pour it in after the other ingredients are layered in the dish.

In a hurry? Buy packaged soft stuffing cubes to save time.

Onion Soufflé

reparation time: 20 minutes
ooking time: about 1 hour,
plus time to make Purée
erves 4 to 6

2 cups Purée Soubise (see Index)
1/2 pound fresh plum tomatoes
2 ounces butter
1/2 cup salted peanuts
2 tablespoons flour
1/2 teaspoon salt
1/4 teaspoon dry mustard
1/2 to 3/4 cup light cream
4 egg yolks
5 egg whites

1. Make **Purée Soubise.** Blanch and peel **tomatoes,** halve them, and scoop out seeds and juice (use for something else). Cut **tomato pulp** into 1/4-inch cubes. Melt 1 tablespoon **butter** in a small saucepan. Add tomatoes and sauté, turning often, until cubes are soft and almost translucent. Gently stir **tomatoes** into the **onion purée.**

2. Use another tablespoon of **butter** to coat the inside of a 6-cup soufflé dish. Crush 2 tablespoons **peanuts** almost to a powder (use mortar and pestle or food processor), and sprinkle these crumbs all over the butter coating.

3. Melt remaining ounce of **butter** in a large saucepan. Off the heat stir in the **flour, salt** and **mustard.** Pour in 1/2 cup of the **cream** and return to low heat. Stir constantly until the mixture forms a thick sauce. Mix in the **onion purée** until well combined. If the sauce is too thick, stir in the rest of the cream.

4. Beat the **egg yolks** until well mixed. Stir in about 1 cup of the onion mixture to warm eggs, then combine **eggs** with the rest of the **sauce.** Let the mixture cool. Chop the rest of the **peanuts.** Preheat oven to 375°F.

5. Beat **egg whites** with a pinch of **salt** until stiff peaks stand straight up when beater is withdrawn. Mix about a third of the whites into the **onion mixture.** Gently fold in the rest.

6. Spoon a third of the **batter** into the prepared dish and gently sprinkle half of the chopped **peanuts** over it. Spoon in another third of the batter and sprinkle with the rest of the peanuts. Spoon in the rest of the batter.

7. Bake the soufflé for 30 minutes for a slightly moist center, 40 minutes for a drier soufflé.

Spanish-Style Lemon Sole with Onions

preparation time: 15 minutes
cooking time: 25 minutes
serves 6

6 fillets of lemon sole, each about 8 ounces
salt
2 pounds large Spanish onions
3 red bell peppers, about 1 pound
1 tablespoon plus 1 teaspoon olive oil
1/2 cup fish stock
3 ounces Spanish white wine
12 green ripe olives

1. Rinse **fillets,** pat dry, and arrange skin side up on a working surface. Split them along the natural division, making 12 narrow pieces. Sprinkle each piece lightly with **salt.**

2. Peel **onions,** halve them from top to bottom, and cut each half into thin slivers. Peel **peppers** with a swivel vegetable peeler and discard stems, ribs and seeds. Cut peppers into thin slivers.

3. Pour 1 tablespoon **oil** into a large skillet and add **onions.** Stir over low heat until onions begin to cook, then pour in 1/4 cup of the **fish stock** and sprinkle with a little **salt.** Cover onions and cook over low heat until they are very tender and golden. Turn them to cook evenly. Toward the end add the **pepper slivers** and continue to cook until tender. Preheat oven to 350°F.

4. Use remaining **oil** to brush on a baking dish and on a sheet of foil large enough to cover it. Arrange about 1 tablespoon **onion shreds** and a few **pepper slivers** on each piece of **fillet** and roll them up. Scrape remaining onion and pepper slivers into the baking dish, and place **fish rolls,** seam side down, on the **vegetables.**

5. Pour remaining **stock** and the **wine** into the baking dish around the fish rolls. Press the sheet of foil, oiled side down, on the fish. Bake in oven for about 15 minutes, until fish is snow white and tender.

6. Serve 2 rolls for each serving. Spoon onions and peppers over, and garnish with **olives.** Serve with steamed new potatoes and a salad of cucumber and fennel.

variation: For a smaller serving, use fillets of smaller flounders, about 4 ounces each, and do not split them. Keep the same weight proportions—3 pounds fish, 2 pounds onions, 1 pound peppers.
Try to find a Spanish white wine that is golden in color, with a taste leaning toward sherry, for the perfect match.

Beef and Onion Stew in Crockpot

Preparation time: 15 minutes
Cooking time: 12 hours
Serves 6 to 8

3 pounds shin of beef, in thick slices
2 pounds small onions, white or yellow, about 2 ounces each
1/2 pound carrots
1/2 pound parsnips
1 teaspoon dried rosemary
salt
1 large bay leaf
6 ounces dry vermouth
1/4 cup chopped fresh coriander

1. Rinse pieces of **beef** and pat dry. Peel **onions.** Scrape **carrots** and **parsnips** and cut into 1-inch chunks.
2. Put all the **vegetables** in the bottom of a crockpot. Sprinkle them with **rosemary** and a little **salt.** Put the **bay leaf** in the center, and on top place the slices of **beef shin.** Pour in **vermouth** and an equal amount of water (3/4 cup).
3. Set the cooker at high and cook for 1 hour. Reduce to low and continue to cook for 11 hours longer.
4. Lift out the **beef slices** and peel off skin. Remove any cartilage or lumps of fat, and the bone in the center of each slice, but save any marrow and add it to the stew. Return the beef to the pot, gently mix all together, and serve sprinkled with **fresh coriander.** Wide egg noodles are perfect with this stew.

variation: This stew can be made in more conventional ways also. In that case, braise the beef for 1 hour before adding onions and other ingredients. You will need more liquid. Increase vermouth to 1 cup and double the water, or use part beef stock.

Chicken with Onions and Cashews

preparation time: 15 minutes
cooking time: 35 to 40 minutes
serves 4

1-1/4 pounds chicken breasts
3 sprigs of celery leaves
1 teaspoon salt
12 ounces pearl onions
1 ounce gingerroot
3 tablespoons vegetable oil
4 ounces unroasted cashews
2 tablespoons rice-wine vinegar
2 pimientos, cut into diamonds

1. Cover **chicken** with cold water, add **celery leaves** and **salt,** and bring to a boil. Simmer for 12 minutes. Let chicken cool in the broth. Save the broth. Remove skin, bones and cartilage from chicken and cut meat into 1-1/2-inch chunks.
2. Blanch and peel **onions.** Return onions to saucepan and add 1 cup of the **chicken broth.** Simmer onions until just tender; drain and set aside.
3. Peel and mince **gingerroot.** Heat **oil** in a large skillet and sauté gingerroot for 3 minutes. With a skimmer lift gingerroot to a plate.
4. Put **chicken pieces** in the skillet and sauté, turning on all sides, for 2 minutes. Add **cashews** and **onions** and cook for 2 minutes longer.
5. Pour in **vinegar** and 1/2 cup of the chicken broth; return gingerroot, and mix well. Simmer the mixture, covered, for about 15 minutes, or until chicken is done to your taste. Cashews will still be crisp. Stir in **pimiento** pieces and serve over rice.

Noodle Casserole with Three Onions

preparation time: 20 minutes
cooking time: 1-1/2 hours
serves 6 to 8

12 ounces pearl onions
2 ounces butter
salt
8 ounces egg noodles
1 pound yellow onions
2 tablespoons olive oil
10 ounces boneless and skinless raw chicken or veal
1/2 cup tomato purée
1/2 cup chicken stock
1 teaspoon ground sage
1 bunch of scallions, about 12

1. Drop unpeeled **pearl onions** into a saucepan, cover with boiling water, and bring again to a boil. Boil for 3 minutes, then pour into a colander and rinse with cold water. Cut off the root end and gently press the onion, it will pop out of the outermost layer of skin. Continue until all are peeled. This can be done a day ahead to save time.

2. Use a teaspoon of the **butter** to coat the inside of a 2-quart casserole, also the inside of the cover or a sheet of foil. Bring a large pot of water to a boil; add 1 tablespoon **salt** and the **noodles.** Cook noodles until al dente, drain well, and turn them into the buttered casserole.

3. While noodles cook, peel and slice **yellow onions.** Melt remaining **butter** in a large skillet and add the **oil.** Sauté **sliced onions** in the skillet, turning them from time to time, until they are golden and beginning to brown on the edges. Use a slotted spoon to transfer them to the casserole of **noodles.** Leave all the oil and butter in the skillet.

4. Add **pearl onions** to the skillet and quickly sauté them, shaking the pan often. Add these to the **noodles,** again leaving any oil in the pan. Preheat oven to 350°F.

5. Trim any fat or cartilage from the **chicken** or **veal,** slice the meat, then cut into 3/4-inch slivers. Sauté the slivers in the skillet until barely browned, then add to the **noodles.**

6. Combine **tomato purée** and **stock** and pour into casserole. Sprinkle with the **sage** and a little **salt** if needed. With 2 wooden spoons or paddles, gently mix until all the ingredients are evenly distributed. Cover the casserole with cover or foil.

7. Bake the casserole for about 1 hour. While it bakes, wash and trim **scallions;** keep about 3 inches of the green part (the rest can be used for stock). Cut scallions across into 1/2-inch rounds. When the casserole is nearly done, sauté scallion rounds in the skillet (add more butter if needed). At serving time, sprinkle **scallions** around the top of the **noodles.**

variations: Lean beef can be used instead of chicken or veal. Or omit meat to have a dish for accompaniment.

For a vegetarian dish, omit meat and substitute white wine or vegetable stock for chicken stock; for a heartier dish, use 8 ounces cheese (Cheddar, Jarlsberg, Munster), shredded.

Everything in this casserole is relative; use more or less noodles, more or less onions, more or less poultry; bake for a longer time at lower temperature, for a shorter time at higher temperature.

Pork Tenderloin with Bean-Thread Noodles

preparation time: 40 minutes
cooking time: 30 to 40 minutes
serves 6 to 8

2 fresh pork tenderloins, about 2 pounds altogether
1 yellow onion, about 3 ounces
2 ounces fresh gingerroot
1 large lemon
2 ounces dry white wine or dry sherry
1-1/2 pounds small white onions (silverskins)
4 ounces bean-thread (cellophane) noodles
2 tablespoons peanut oil or light vegetable oil
1-1/2 cups chicken stock or pork broth
2 tablespoons light soy sauce

1. Trim **tenderloins** of fat and tendons, and cut across into medallions about 1/2 inch thick. Place the pieces in a large pottery or glass container.
2. Peel and chop **yellow onion** and **gingerroot,** and drop pieces into the bowl of a food processor fitted with the steel blade. Use a swivel vegetable peeler to remove the outer yellow rind of the **lemon,** and add rind pieces to the processor. Pour in the **wine** and process to make a thick marinade. Pour over the **pork,** turn pieces to coat them all, and let them marinate for about 30 minutes.
3. Trim roots from **white onions,** cut a cross in the root end of each one, and cover with boiling water. Bring to a boil, then simmer for 10 to 12 minutes, until onions are half tender. Drain, and rinse with cold water. When cool enough to handle, peel the **onions.**
4. Pour boiling water over **bean-thread noodles** and let them stand until water reaches room temperature. Drain noodles, spread them out on a cutting board, and cut into 3-inch lengths.
5. Remove **pork medallions** from marinade and pat dry. Heat **oil** in a large skillet or wok and sauté pork pieces, a few at a time, until browned on both sides. Remove them to a plate and continue until all are browned.
6. In the **oil** remaining in the skillet, sauté the **white onions** until beginning to brown. Pour in **stock** or **broth** and bring to a boil. Stir in remaining **marinade** and the **juice of the lemon.** Bring to a simmer.
7. Return **pork medallions** to the pan and simmer until pork is fully cooked and onions tender, about 15 minutes. Add drained **noodles,** bring to a boil again, and remove from heat. Stir in **soy sauce** and serve.

Veal à la Madeleine

aration time: 10 minutes
ing time: 30 to 40 minutes
s 6

1 red bell pepper, 6 to 8 ounces
1 pound yellow onions
2 ounces butter
1 tablespoon olive oil
salt and white pepper
6 veal grenadins (slices cut from the round or tenderloin) or boned chops
3 ounces dry white wine or Madeira
6 slices of Fontina or Havarti cheese
6 lemon slices
paprika

Make this for a dinner party; it is easy and quick to prepare and has elegance in taste and appearance.

1. Use a swivel vegetable peeler to peel the **pepper;** or char it under the broiler and remove blackened skin. Trim pepper, discard stem, ribs and seeds, and cut into small dice. Peel and chop **onions.**
2. Melt half of the **butter** with half of the **oil** in a skillet. Sauté the **pepper pieces** until tender; with a slotted spoon transfer them to a plate. Put **onions** in the skillet and sauté over low heat, stirring often, until onions are very soft and tender. If the pan begins to dry before onions are tender, add a few tablespoons of water. Season onions with **salt** and **white pepper** and mix in the **red pepper pieces.** Spoon the vegetable mixture onto a plate. Preheat broiler.
3. Use the rest of the **oil** to coat a shallow baking dish large enough to hold all 6 veal pieces in a single layer. Melt the rest of the **butter** in the skillet and sauté the **veal pieces** on both sides until just golden, about 2 minutes on each side. Transfer veal pieces to the oiled baking dish.
4. Deglaze the skillet with **white wine** or **Madeira** and let the wine reduce to half. Return **onions** to the skillet, mix, then divide the wine and vegetable mixture among the **veal grenadins,** piling it in an even layer. Arrange a **cheese slice** on top.
5. Slide the baking dish under the broiler and broil until the **cheese** melts. Meanwhile, sprinkle each **lemon slice** with **paprika** and garnish each serving with 1 slice.

45

Onion and Rice Stuffing

preparation time: about 20
minutes
cooking time: about 1-1/2
hours
makes 8 to 10 cups

2 pounds large onions
oil
1-1/2 cups uncooked rice
salt
2 lemons
8 ounces dried apricots
2 ounces butter
chopped herbs (optional)

This stuffing is good with turkey, chicken and Cornish game hens. It makes enough for a 10-pound turkey, two 5-pound chickens, and at least 8 Cornish hens. Or it can be baked separately.

1. Pierce the **unpeeled onions** with a skewer and brush lightly with **oil.** Bake them in a 375°F. oven for about 1 hour. When cool enough to handle, peel and chop them.
2. While onions bake, put **rice** in a 2-quart saucepan with 3 cups **water** and 1 teaspoon **salt.** Grate the **lemon rind** and set it aside. Squeeze the **lemons.** Add 2 tablespoons of the **juice** to the **rice.** Bring rice to a boil and simmer until all the water is absorbed. Rice will be about two-thirds cooked.
3. Put **apricots** in a bowl. Bring 2 cups **water** to a boil and pour it into the apricots. Let them soak until water cools. Reserve the water. Cut apricots into pieces with kitchen scissors.
4. Melt **butter** in a large saucepan and sauté chopped **onions** until golden. Stir in **apricots, rice,** remaining **lemon juice** and grated **lemon rind.** Mix well. Taste; you may want to add more **salt.** Add a few tablespoons of **chopped herbs** if you like (parsley, mint, savory, thyme). If stuffing is too dry, stir in some of the liquid used for soaking apricots. Orange juice or chicken stock can be used also. The mixture should be moist but not soupy. Let the stuffing cool before filling poultry.

variations: The livers of the birds can be added. Poach them briefly, then cut up before mixing in.
Pine nuts are delicious added to this, but very expensive.
A stuffing without apricots can be flavored with ground sage; without fruits you will need to add at least 1 cup chicken stock to have enough liquid.

Onion Toast

paration time: 10 minutes
king time: 15 minutes
es 4

2 large Spanish onions, about 1 pound altogether
2 ounces butter
4 large slices of French bread
salt and pepper
3 ounces Cheddar cheese
4 teaspoons prepared mustard

1. Peel **onions,** cut off small portions at top and bottom (use for something else) and cut the rest into thin slices. Melt half of the **butter** in a skillet and gently sauté onion slices until lightly browned.

2. Cut the **bread** on the diagonal to make rather large slices. Toast them in a toaster or under the broiler until just golden. Use remaining **butter** to spread on toast.

3. Divide **onion slices** among the **bread slices,** making a rather thick layer, and sprinkle with **salt** and **pepper.** Slice or shred the **cheese** and place on top of the onions in an even layer. Spread 1 teaspoon **mustard,** whatever kind you like, on each sandwich.

4. Place toasts on a baking sheet and slide under the broiler, placing the rack about 5 inches from the heat source. Broil until **cheese** is melting. Fresh tomato salad is good with this; it makes a fine lunch on a cool day.

variation: Onion Canapés. Follow the procedure used for onion toast. Allow 1 onion slice and 1 cheese slice for each canapé. Make the bases from firm white or rye bread; cut rounds with a cutter the same size as the onion slices. Toast and butter the rounds. Place an onion slice and a cheese slice on each round. Mix equal parts of mild mustard and mayonnaise and spread about 1/3 teaspoon on each canapé. These can be assembled ahead. Broil them only just before serving. Make them fancier with parsley sprigs or capers.

Chicken, Onion and Avocado Salad

preparation time: 30 minutes,
plus time to cool chicken
cooking time: 15 minutes
serves 6

2 pounds chicken breasts
salt
1 thick sprig of celery leaves
1 small yellow onion, stuck with 1 clove
1 pound Bermuda onions
2 avocados
juice of 1 lemon
8 ounces tender celery ribs
1 pound curly chicory or other salad greens
1/2 teaspoon dry mustard
2 ounces Sauterne
6 tablespoons light olive oil
black pepper

This is a pretty and delicious dish for a party luncheon.

1. Halve the **chicken breasts** and put in a saucepan with 1 teaspoon **salt,** the **celery leaves** and the small **yellow onion.** Just cover with water and bring to a simmer. Poach the chicken for about 15 minutes, until it tests done. Let it cool in the liquid.

2. When **chicken** is cold, discard skin, bones and cartilage, and cut the meat into 3/4-inch chunks. Cover and set aside in a cool place.

3. Peel **Bermuda onions,** slice, and separate slices into rings. Cover with ice water and let them soak for 15 minutes. Peel **avocados,** halve them, remove pits, and cut the fruit into 3/4-inch chunks. Pour the **lemon juice** over the pieces and toss to coat all surfaces. Cover avocados with plastic wrap.

4. Wash and dry **celery ribs** and cut them across into 1/2-inch crescents. Wash **chicory,** drain well, and roll in a towel to dry.

5. Stir **dry mustard** and 1 teaspoon **salt** into the **Sauterne** until dissolved. Mix in the **olive oil.**

6. To assemble the salad, spread **chicory** on a salad platter or divide among 6 salad plates. In a bowl combine the **chicken, avocado** and **celery pieces.** Mix the **dressing** well, then pour into the bowl and toss to mix. Finally, drain the **onion rings** and pat dry. Add these to the salad and toss gently to keep them whole. Spoon the salad onto the greens and grind a little **black pepper** over it.

variation: Instead of wine in the dressing, use the same amount of fresh orange juice, or half as much lemon juice.

Onion and Olive Salad

eparation time: about 30
minutes
rves 6

3 red onions, each about 6 ounces
salt
1 cup pitted black olives
2 Belgian endives
1 bunch watercress
2 tablespoons lemon juice
1/4 teaspoon dry mustard
1/4 cup olive oil

1. Peel **onions,** cut into crosswise slices, and put in a bowl. Taste a piece; some red onions are very sharp. If they are sharp, sprinkle generously with **salt,** being sure each slice is salted, and let them soak until onions begin to release juices. Then rinse off the salt, and pat dry. If the onions are mild, soak them in ice water for 15 minutes, then drain and pat dry.

2. Rinse and dry **olives** and cut into crosswise slices. Wash **endives,** remove any damaged outer leaves, and scoop out the core at the base. Cut endives into thin slivers. Wash **watercress** thoroughly, roll in a towel to dry, and gently toss with **endive slivers.** Make a bed of the greens on a platter or on 6 salad plates.

3. Pour **lemon juice** into a small bowl. Dissolve **mustard** and 1 teaspoon **salt** in juice, then beat in the **oil.** Pour **dressing** over the **onions** and gently toss until all pieces are coated. Mix in the **olives.** Arrange the mixture over the **greens,** or divide among the individual salad plates. Serve as a salad course, or as accompaniment to pasta or meat loaf, or use as a first course with Italian bread and cheese.

variation: Use more dressing if you prefer. If you use vinegar instead of lemon juice, increase the amount of oil to 6 tablespoons for better taste balance.

Japanese Onion Salad

preparation time: 45 minutes
cooking time: 2 or 3 minutes to
    toast sesame seeds
serves 4

1 pound yellow onions or Bermuda onions
2 teaspoons sea salt crystals
1/4 cup white sesame seeds
1/4 cup soy sauce
1/4 cup rice-wine vinegar

1. Peel the **onions,** then halve them from stem to blossom end. Continuing
to slice from top to bottom, cut each half into thin wedges. Place wedges in
a bowl, sprinkle with **sea salt,** and cover with ice water. Soak Bermuda
onions for 10 minutes, yellow onions for 30 minutes.
2. Drain and rinse **onions** and pat dry. Rinse and dry the bowl, and return
onions to the bowl. Toast **sesame seeds** in a dry skillet until they begin to
jump in the pan. Transfer to a mortar and crush them. (Or scrape into a food
processor fitted with the steel blade, add soy sauce and vinegar, and
process until seeds are ground.)
3. Pour **sesame seeds, soy sauce** and **vinegar** over onions and mix gently. Let
them soak to absorb flavors for at least 15 minutes. At serving time spoon
onions and **dressing** into 4 small bowls. Serve with rice or other grains, or
with fish. While it is not a very Japanese combination, this salad tastes great
with hamburgers.

variation: Instead of soaking raw onions, sauté the slices in sesame oil for
about 15 minutes, until tender and lighly browned. Add the mixture of
sesame seeds, soy sauce and rice-wine vinegar, and add 1 teaspoon finely
ground sea salt. Serve in bowls.

Baghdad Onion Relish

preparation time: 40 minutes
makes about 3 cups

2 Bermuda onions, each about 8 ounces
2 teaspoons sea salt crystals
2 limes
12 fresh mint leaves

Serve this with other dishes as an hors-d'oeuvre, or as a salad, a relish, or a cold vegetable with salads or aspic dishes.

1. Peel **onions,** cut them into 1/3-inch slices, and arrange them in a large shallow bowl. Sprinkle **sea salt** crystals over them, then gently cover them with ice water. Let them soak for 30 minutes, then drain, rinse, and gently pat dry. Rinse and dry the bowl and return onions to it.
2. Grate **lime rind** and set aside. Squeeze **juice** from the limes and sprinkle it over the **onions.** Wash and dry **mint leaves** and cut them into tiny slivers. Sprinkle **lime rind** and **mint** over **onions,** and let them rest for 10 minutes before serving.

variation: Use lemons if limes are not available, and dried mint if fresh is out of season.

Onion and Pepper Relish

preparation time: about 40
minutes
cooking time: about 10
minutes to char peppers
makes 3 to 4 cups

2 Bermuda onions, each about 8 ounces
2 teaspoons sea salt
3 green peppers, each about 6 ounces
2 hot red peppers
1 teaspoon ground coriander
1/2 cup basil or tarragon vinegar or white-wine vingegar
1 cup dairy sour cream

1. Peel and slice **onions.** Put them in a pottery or glass dish, sprinkle with the **sea salt,** and cover with ice water. Let them stand for about 20 minutes.
2. Wash and trim **green peppers.** Roast them in the oven or char under the broiler until skin is black. Remove skin and discard stems, ribs and seeds. Cut **peppers** into strips.
3. Wearing rubber or plastic gloves, slit **hot peppers,** rinse off seeds, and discard stems and ribs. Chop hot peppers and mix with green peppers. Wash gloves before removing them.
4. Drain **onions** and mix with **peppers.** Sprinkle with **coriander** and pour in **vinegar.** Let the mixture marinate for about 10 minutes.
5. Stir in **sour cream** and mix gently until well combined. Serve with fish, shellfish, and curries.

Three Scallion Garnishes

1. SCALLION BRUSHES: These are part of the service of Peking duck, but they can be used to garnish many other dishes, even as part of a selection of raw vegetables for hors-d'oeuvre. Wash and trim **scallions** and cut all to 3-inch lengths, including some of the green leaves or not as you prefer. Leaving half of the length uncut, split the rest into quarters, making a sort of fringe. Soak the brushes in ice water until the cut ends curl. One of these brushes is used to spread duck sauce on each doily (a thin pancake) used to wrap a piece of duck. The scallion is eaten with the duck and doily.

2. SCALLIONS AND GINGERROOT: This mixture is added to Chinese chicken, beef or shellfish dishes. Wash and trim **scallions** and cut across into thin rings, including the green part. Peel **gingerroot** and mince. Sauté the mixture in **vegetable oil,** then add to the main ingredient. Or cut scallions into 1-inch lengths and gingerroot into thin slices. Sauté gingerroot, but stir in scallion pieces just before serving.

3. SCALLION GREMOLATA: This mixture is for those unlucky people allergic to garlic, which is usual in gremolata. Wash and trim 6 **scallions** and 10 **parsley sprigs.** Dry them both. Peel off the yellow rind (zest) of 2 **lemons.** Mince all together until well combined. Or chop in a food processor fitted with the steel blade; first chop lemon rind with quick on and off turns, then add scallions and parsley and process until minced. Sprinkle on braised meats.

Two Onion Garnishes

1. LYONNAISE: This term on a menu indicates a garnish of sautéed onions. Onions may be minced or sliced. For each 1/2 pound **onions** use 2 ounces **butter,** and sauté them until golden brown.
For **Lyonnaise Potatoes,** use 1 pound **potatoes** and 1/2 pound **onions;** sauté them separately, then combine, season, sprinkle with **parsley.**
For **Chicken Lyonnaise,** add the sautéed **onions** to half-cooked **chicken** also sautéed in **butter** and finish cooking them together. Transfer chicken to a serving dish, add a little chicken or veal gravy to the onions, reduce, season, and spoon over the chicken. Sprinkle with **parsley.**
For **Omelet Lyonnaise,** use 2 ounces minced **onion** for 3 **eggs.** Sauté onion in 1 tablespoon **butter** until browned; beat the eggs with seasoning and chopped **parsley,** pour into the onion, and cook until done to your taste.

2. TEX-MEX: This small salad is used to garnish beef and bean dishes, bean salads, tacos, tostadas, and other Mexican-style sandwiches made with tortillas as the bread.
Measure equal weights of Bermuda or Spanish **onions,** ripe **tomatoes** and **avocados,** and half the weight of **iceberg lettuce** and **yellow cheese** (Cheddar, Monterey Jack, etc.). Peel **onions** and **avocados; tomatoes** can be peeled or not as you prefer. Cut vegetables and **lettuce** into small cubes; shred the **cheese.** Toss all together. Season the mixture at the last minute. Spoon onto the beef, beans, tortillas, etc., before serving.

Pickled Onions

preparation time: 30 to 40 minutes, plus overnight soaking
cooking time: about 20 minutes
makes 1 pint

1 pound pearl onions
2 tablespoons sea salt crystals
1/2 ounce fresh gingerroot
2 cups white vinegar
6 tablespoons sugar
1 large bay leaf
2 teaspoons fennel seeds
1 teaspoon black peppercorns
1 teaspoon red pepper flakes

The ingredients given here will make only a small amount of pickle. If you have more pearl onions and the patience to peel them, increase everything in the same proportions, but have some extra vinegar in reserve if you are making large amounts.

1. Drop **onions** into a large pot of boiling water and boil for 3 minutes. Drain, rinse with cold water, and drain again. Cut off the root ends and pop onions out of the peel. Put them in a bowl, sprinkle with the **salt,** and just cover with cold water. Let them stand overnight.

2. Next day pour off the water, rinse onions with cold water, and put them in a stainless-steel or enamelware saucepan. Peel **gingerroot,** mince or sliver it, and add to onions.

3. Pour **vinegar** into another similar saucepan. Over low heat stir in **sugar** until dissolved. Add the **bay leaf.** Crush all the **spices** lightly and add. Bring vinegar to a boil and simmer for 10 minutes.

4. Pour **vinegar** through a fine strainer into **onions,** bring again to a boil, and simmer for 10 minutes. Spoon **onions** into a sterilized pint jar and pour in enough of the spiced **vinegar** to cover them completely, which is usually all of it. When cool, refrigerate.

note: I have made these with tiny red onions. After soaking all night, they become blue! When they have simmered with the vinegar, they become an exquisite rosy-red color.

If the onions are very tiny, they need only 2 minutes or less boiling before peeling, and only 7 or 8 minutes in the pickling solution. However, there's more work with the tiny ones.

This is a very "hot" pickle. For a milder version, omit the ginger entirely, and halve the amount of black peppercorns and red pepper flakes. For a slightly sweeter pickle, increase sugar to 8 tablespoons.

Irish Onion Sauce

paration time: 10 minutes
king time: about 20
    minutes
es about 2-1/2 cups sauce

2 pounds yellow onions
1 small white turnip
2 cups milk
2 cups water
1-1/2 ounces butter, softened
1 teaspoon salt
pinch of white pepper
pinch of grated nutmeg
1/2 cup sweet cream or dairy sour cream

1. Peel **onions,** quarter them, and drop into a heavy saucepan. Peel the **turnip,** halve it, and add to onions. (Turnip is supposed to make onions less acid.) Add **milk** and **water,** bring to a simmer, and cook over low heat for 15 to 20 minutes, until onions are very soft.

2. Lift out and discard the **turnip pieces.** Use a skimmer to transfer **onions** to the bowl of a food processor fitted with the steel blade, or to the container of a blender. Add the soft **butter** and **seasoning** and process until onions are puréed. If the purée is very thick, add a little of the cooking liquid.

3. Pour **purée** into a clean saucepan and stir in the **cream.** Heat to serving temperature, but do not let the sauce boil lest it curdle. Serve with duck, goose or rabbit, or beef steaks. Vegetarians like this with baked bulgur (cracked wheat) or steamed kasha.

French Onion Sauce (Sauce Soubise)

preparation time: 15 minutes
cooking time: 30 to 40 minutes
makes about 3 cups sauce

2 pounds yellow onions
4 ounces butter
2 tablespoons all-purpose flour, sifted
salt and white pepper
1 cup chicken or veal stock
light cream (optional)

This onion sauce was named for Charles de Rohan, Prince de Soubise, a marshal of France, prominent at the court of Louis XV.

1. Peel and mince **onions.** Put them in a deep saucepan, cover with boiling water, and set the pot over moderate heat for 3 minutes. Drain well, turn onions out on a thick layer of cloth towels, and pat as dry as possible.
2. Melt 2 ounces of the **butter** in the dried saucepan and cook the **onions** in it for at least 10 minutes, or until they are very soft. Stir in the **flour, salt** to taste, and a little **white pepper.** When well mixed, pour in the **stock** and simmer for 15 to 30 minutes.
3. Push the mixture through a sieve, or purée through a food mill into another saucepan, and bring to serving temperature. Add a few tablespoons **cream** if the purée is too thick. Remove from heat and stir in remaining **butter;** it should melt in the retained heat of the sauce. Serve with poultry, pork, eggs.

Purée Soubise

paration time: 15 minutes
king time: 1 hour
kes about 4 cups sauce

2 pounds yellow onions
4 ounces butter
1/2 pound long-grain white rice
3 cups chicken or veal stock
salt·
1/4 cup light cream

1. Prepare **onions** as in Step 1 for Sauce Soubise. Melt 2 ounces of the **butter** in a saucepan and stir in onions over low heat until they begin to cook.
2. Stir in **rice** and **stock** and about 1 teaspoon **salt** (the exact amount depends on the saltiness of the stock). Bring to a simmer and cook over very low heat for almost 1 hour. The rice should be very soft.
3. Put everything—**onions, rice, stock**—through a food mill into a clean saucepan. Taste and add more **salt** if needed. Stir in the **cream,** then remaining **butter.**
4. This makes a thick sauce, but it is more often used as an accompaniment or garnish. Serve with poultry, veal or lamb.

Sauce Robert

paration time: 15 minutes
king time: 40 minutes, plus
    time to prepare demi-
    glace sauce
kes about 3 cups sauce

2 pounds yellow onions
2 ounces butter
1 cup dry white wine
1 cup demi-glace sauce (reduced Sauce Espagnole/Brown Sauce)
2 tablespoons prepared Dijon mustard

1. Peel and mince **onions.** Put them in a deep saucepan, cover with boiling water, and set the pot over moderate heat for 3 minutes. Drain well and pat dry.
2. Melt **butter** in the dried saucepan and cook the **onions** in it for about 5 minutes, until they are soft. Pour in the **wine** and cook over low heat until reduced by one third. Pour in the **demi-glace sauce** and simmer for 20 minutes.
3. Purée the sauce through a sieve or food mill into another saucepan, and stir in the **mustard.** Bring to serving temperature, then set the pan in a hot-water bath to keep it warm. Do not let sauce reach boiling after it is finished. Serve with pork.

note: Demi-glace sauce is available in jars at good food markets.

Green Onion Butter

preparation time: 15 minutes
cooking time: 3 minutes to
blanch scallions
makes about 2 cups, 10 to 12
servings

2 bunches of scallions, about 24
salt
1/2 pound unsalted butter
1/2 cup medium-dry white wine
lemon juice (optional)
2 tablespoons minced parsley

Especially good for broccoli, cauliflower, asparagus, but also delicious on broiled chicken, sautéed veal, and even steamed new potatoes.

1. Wash and trim **scallions;** keep about 3 inches of the green part (the rest can be used for soup or stock). Cut scallions into thin rounds, put them in a saucepan, and cover with boiling water. Add a few pinches of **salt** and simmer scallions for 3 minutes. Drain, rinse with cold water, and drain again.
2. While the scallions are blanching, let the **butter** reach room temperature. Try not to let it melt. With a wooden spoon cream it, as if starting to make a cake, until it is almost white and very fluffy. Beat in the **wine;** you may prefer to use a whisk when adding the wine. Finally beat in the well-drained **scallions.**
3. Taste; add as much **salt** as you need, but be sure to beat it in so it is dissolved and not grainy. If the butter needs more zip, add a few drops of **lemon juice.** Just before serving, mix in **parsley.** Serve at room temperature, or cold. If it is served hot, the butter will melt, but that is also delicious.

variation: If you have a food processor, blanch whole scallions before cutting them up, then chop them in the machine. If you do not plan to serve this the day it is made, blanch the parsley also, rinse with cold water, and pat dry before mixing it into the butter. Use this butter within 2 days for best flavor.

58

Peanut Butter and Onion Sandwiches

:paration time: 10 minutes
ves 6

12 slices of whole-wheat bread
1 tablespoon butter
4 ounces peanut butter
1 Bermuda onion, about 8 ounces
salt and pepper
2 tablespoons minced parsley
3 tablespoons mayonnaise

1. Lay out the **bread slices** and spread six of them with 1/2 teaspoon **butter** each. Cover the buttered slices with **peanut butter,** spreading to the edge all around.

2. Peel the **onion** and cut across into 6 thin slices. Place 1 slice on top of peanut butter layer. Sprinkle with **salt** and **pepper,** and cover the onion with 1 teaspoon minced **parsley.**

3. Spread 1/2 tablespoon **mayonnaise** on each of the 6 unbuttered slices, and place them on top of the onions. With a sharp knife cut the **sandwiches** into halves, either across or diagonally, and place on a luncheon plate.

4. Garnish each plate with a few ripple potato chips, a dill pickle spear, and a parsley sprig.

Onion Rolls

preparation time: 40 minutes,
plus 1 to 2 hours for rising
cooking time: 20 minutes for
onions, 30 minutes for
baking
makes 20 rolls or 10 sandwich
rolls

1 cup fresh or sour milk
1 teaspoon salt
2-1/2 ounces butter
1/4 cup warm water (105° to 115°F.)
1 teaspoon sugar
1 package active dry yeast (7 grams)
4 to 5 cups unbleached flour
1 egg, well beaten
oil
1 pound yellow onions
1 teaspoon ground sage
2 ounces Romano cheese
1 egg yolk (optional)
1/4 cup poppy seeds (optional)

1. Combine the **milk, salt** and 1 ounce of the **butter** in a saucepan and set over low heat until salt is dissolved and butter melted. Cool to warm (105° to 115°F.).

2. Pour 1/4 cup **warm water** into a large mixing bowl and sprinkle in **sugar** and **yeast.** Stir. When yeast is dissolved, pour in the **milk mixture** and 4 cups **flour.** Mix until flour is moistened, then stir in the **whole egg** and beat with a wooden spoon until a dough is formed.

3. Turn **dough** out on a clean smooth surface and knead for about 6 minutes, until it is smooth, stretchy, no longer sticking to hands or surface. Add some of the last cup of **flour** if needed, but the rolls are lighter with only 4 cups flour.

4. Wash and dry the mixing bowl and pour in 1 teaspoon **oil.** Put the ball of **dough** in the bowl and turn to coat with oil on all sides. Cover with a sheet of wax paper, then with a damp towel, and set in a warm place (75° to 85°F.) to rise for 1 hour, until doubled in bulk.

5. While dough rises, peel and mince **onions;** they should be almost puréed. Melt remaining **butter** in a skillet and sauté onions until they are rather dry and beginning to brown on the edges. Stir in the **sage,** mix well, and let the mixture cool. Finally grate the **cheese** and stir into the **onions.**

6. Punch down the **dough,** divide into halves, and work with half at a time. Roll out the dough to a rectangle about 12 inches on the long sides, and spread it with half of the **onion mixture,** leaving the long edges bare. Roll up from one long side to a tight roll. Cut into 10 triangles. Roll out, fill, and cut the second half in the same way.

7. Use 1 teaspoon **oil** each to coat 2 baking sheets, and place 10 rolls on each one, allowing ample space between them. Cover with wax paper and a damp towel and let them rise again for 30 to 45 minutes, until doubled.

8 Preheat oven to 350°F. while rolls are rising. If you like the tops glazed and seeded, beat the **egg yolk** with 1 tablespoon **water** and gently brush it over the tops of the rolls. Sprinkle them with **poppy seeds,** using about 1/2 teaspoon for each roll. Bake them for about 30 minutes, until well puffed and golden.

9. For **sandwich rolls:** In Step 6 roll out the halves of dough, spread onion filling on one sheet, and cover with the second. Use a 4-inch cutter to cut out large rolls; usually you can make 10. If the sheet of dough is very thin, you can make 12. Follow Steps 7 and 8.

note: To sour fresh milk, add 1 teaspoon lemon juice to 1 cup milk, stir well and let stand at room temperature for 30 minutes.

Saffron Onion Bread

preparation time: 40 minutes,
plus about 2 hours for
rising
cooking time: 20 minutes for
onions, 1 hour for baking
makes 2 large loaves

1 pound yellow onions
3 ounces butter
1 teaspoon salt
1 teaspoon ground mace
1/4 teaspoon ground cuminseed
grated rind of 2 lemons
1 tablespoon loosely packed whole saffron
2 cups water
2 packages active dry yeast (7 grams each)
2 teaspoons sugar
7 to 8 cups unbleached flour
oil

This pale golden loaf is good plain or toasted; it makes a good partner for fish or ham, either as accompaniment or for a sandwich.

1. Peel and mince **onions;** they should be almost puréed. Melt 2 ounces of the **butter** in a large skillet and sauté onions, stirring often, until they are golden and almost dry. Off the heat sprinkle in the **salt, spices** and **lemon rind,** and mix well. Set aside to cool.
2. While onions are cooking, spoon **saffron** into a heatproof bowl. Bring 1-1/2 cups of the **water** to a boil and pour it over the saffron. Let it rest until it cools to 115°F., then strain the liquid into a clean bowl with a pouring spout.
3. Heat remaining 1/2 cup **water** to warm (105° to 115°F.). Sprinkle **yeast** and **sugar** into a large mixing bowl and pour in the **warm water.** Stir to dissolve yeast and sugar.
4. When **yeast mixture** becomes bubbly, pour in the strained **saffron liquid.** Add the **flour,** 2 cups at a time, alternating with part of the **onion mixture.** Pour the seventh cup of flour onto a clean smooth surface for kneading. Stir the mixture in the bowl with a wooden spoon until all the flour is moistened and the dough pulls from the sides of the bowl.

5. Dump the **dough** onto the kneading surface and knead for 12 minutes, incorporating the seventh cup of flour as you knead. Use an additional cup, or part of it, only if the dough remains sticky. Dough should be smooth and should not stick to hands or kneading surface.

6. Wash and dry mixing bowl, **oil** it, and turn the ball of **dough** in it to coat all sides. Cover with a sheet of wax paper, then with a damp towel, and let rise for 1 hour, or until doubled.

7. Punch **dough** down and turn it over in the bowl. Let it rise again for about 30 minutes.

8. Punch **dough** down again, then turn out and divide into 2 portions. Shape each one into a loaf and fit into an oiled bread pan (9 × 5 × 3 inches). Let rise again until doubled. Preheat oven to 350°F.

9. Melt remaining 1 ounce **butter** and brush the tops of the loaves. Bake them for about 1 hour, until they test done. Remove **loaves** from pans and cool on their sides. Each loaf will weigh about 1-3/4 pounds.

variation: Make 6 small loaves, or 1 large loaf and 3 small loaves, using pans about 6 × 3 × 2 inches. Small loaves will weigh about 10 ounces each.

Index